Democratic Values and the Currency

A lecture given to the Institute of Economic Affairs at Church House, Westminster, on Wednesday 14 January 1998

Rt Hon Michael Portillo

With a postscript by

Martin Feldstein
Professor of Economics, Harvard University

Published by the Institute of Economic Affairs 1998

First published in February 1998 by
The Institute of Economic Affairs
2 Lord North Street
Westminster
London SW1P 3LB

© The Institute of Economic Affairs 1998

Occasional Paper 103
All rights reserved
ISSN 0073-909X
ISBN 0-255 36412-1

Printed in Great Britain by
Hartington Fine Arts Limited, Lancing, West Sussex
Set in Times Roman 11 on 13 point

Contents

Foreword *Professor Colin Robinson* 5

The Author 7

Democratic Values and the Currency 9

1 **Introduction** 9

2 **The Cost and Causes of War** 9

3 **The Ideal of a United Europe** 10

British Policy on European Security 11

Different Models for Europe 12

4 **The Spread of Democracy - and of Security** 13

What is Democracy? 14

Scottish Frustration 15

5 **The Single Currency** 16

Transfer of Monetary and Financial Policy Inevitable 17

The Scope for Autonomy 18

6 **Why Democracy Will Not Work at the European Level** 19

Diversity of European Peoples 20

Looking Back Instead of Forward 20

Big (Global) Competition, Bigger State? 21

7 **Will the Single Currency Be an Economic Success for Britain?** 22

Case for Joining Weaker 23

'Grave Danger' 23

3

8   The Real Questions of Security   25

    The EU's Remaining Security Tasks   25

9   Conclusion   26

    Postscript   Martin Feldstein   29

Foreword

FOR SEVERAL YEARS NOW, the Institute has had a programme of publications, lectures, working lunches and conferences on European issues. Prominent in this programme has been discussion of Economic and Monetary Union (EMU) in Europe - a matter not just of economics but one with very important political implications, as authors of recent IEA papers have pointed out.[1]

In Occasional Paper 103, the Institute is publishing, as part of this series, an original and thought-provoking lecture given by the Rt. Hon. Michael Portillo at Church House, Westminster, on 14 January 1998. Mr Portillo directly addresses the political issues raised by EMU by considering the impact on democracy of a monetary union which precedes political union and setting out the subsequent effects. He examines in detail the single currency as it is seen by our European partners

'...as a project in re-shaping the way our Continent is governed, to create a political union that can free Europe from the fear of conflict between the nations.'

He finds the project likely to produce results which are the opposite of those intended. Democracy will suffer. Transferring decision-making away from '...democratic member-states to the undemocratic European Union' will not promote harmony and security. Instead it is '...highly dangerous, because disillusion and grievance provide a breeding ground for nationalism and extremism'. Mr Portillo therefore urges that '...we should turn from the headlong rush towards European political integration, in which the single currency is a decisive step'.

A recent article in *Time* magazine by the distinguished American economist, Professor Martin Feldstein (former Chairman of the US Council of Economic Advisers), reaches very similar conclusions to Mr Portillo's, though by a different route. Professor Feldstein

---

[1] For example, Otmar Issing, *Europe: Political Union Through Common Money*, Occasional Paper 98, February 1996; Symposium on 'European Monetary Union', *Economic Affairs*, Vol.16 No.3, Summer 1996; and Pedro Schwartz, *Back From the Brink: An Appeal to Fellow Europeans Over Monetary Union*, Occasional Paper 101, January 1997.

rejects the idea that US success with a single currency is relevant to Europe and argues that EMU will lead to an increased European inflation rate. Moreover, like Mr Portillo, his view is that '...a European political union is more likely to be a source of conflict than a foundation for European harmony.' As a complement to Mr Portillo's lecture, we therefore reproduce, by permission of *Time* magazine, Professor Feldstein's article.

As in all Institute publications, the conclusions in this Occasional Paper are those of the authors, not of the Institute (which has no corporate view), its Trustees, Advisers or Directors. It is published as a stimulating contribution to the debate about the future direction of the European Union.

February 1998   COLIN ROBINSON

Editorial Director, The Institute of Economic Affairs
Professor of Economics, University of Surrey

The Author

MICHAEL PORTILLO was Secretary of State for Defence from 1995 to 1997.

He was born in 1953 and attended Harrow County Grammar School for Boys, and Peterhouse, Cambridge, where he gained a first class honours degree in History.

He worked at Conservative Central Office from 1976 to 1979, then spent two years as Special Adviser to the Secretary of State for Energy, followed, after a break, by two years with Kerr-McGee Oil UK.

In 1983 he returned to politics as Special Adviser to the Chancellor of the Exchequer, Nigel Lawson, and in 1984 was elected to Parliament for the Enfield Southgate constituency. Mr Portillo joined the Government as a Whip in 1986, was Parliamentary Under-Secretary in the Department of Health and Social Security from 1987-88, Minister of State for Transport 1988-90, and Minister of State for Local Government 1990-92.

In 1992 he was appointed to the Cabinet as Chief Secretary to the Treasury. In 1994 he became Secretary of State for Employment and in 1995 Secretary of State for Defence, a post he held until the 1997 General Election.

Mr Portillo is currently mixing business interests with writing, speaking engagements, and media work, as well as continuing to play his part in the Conservative Party.

Democratic Values and the Currency
RT HON MICHAEL PORTILLO

1. Introduction

I AM HONOURED to be able to deliver a lecture to the IEA, and I thank John Blundell for the invitation to do so. The triumvirate of Antony Fisher, Arthur Seldon and Ralph Harris has provided a remarkable demonstration of the power and influence of ideas. They patiently expounded a remarkable combination of common sense and academic excellence; never afraid to yell out from the crowd, when, as was usually the case, the ruling emperor of conventional wisdom was actually wearing no clothes. Their thinking deeply affected the last Conservative government, many other governments around the world, and new Labour. I cannot think of a better forum in which to deliver what follows.

My object is to discuss the single currency, but not as it is often talked of in Britain, as though it were merely an economic device which can be measured in terms of costs and benefits. I wish to examine it in the terms used by our partners, who see it as a project in re-shaping the way our Continent is governed, to create a political union that can free Europe from the fear of conflict between the nations.

2. The Cost and Causes of War

IN THE LAST TWO CENTURIES the peoples of Europe have paid a terrible price in wars. In the First World War, 15 million were killed, mainly soldiers. In the Second World War, the toll was at least 41 million, of whom most were civilians. Those terrible events have naturally and rightly led highly distinguished statesmen to dedicate their lives to creating conditions in which war would not occur again. There is no higher or more important objective for politicians in Europe than to work for policies that may better guarantee the security of our Continent and avoid a repetition of the dreadful slaughter of our modern history.

We can distinguish two causes at the root of past conflicts in Europe. The first is Franco-German rivalry. Prussia and Austria invaded France in 1793 and 1813. France occupied Prussian and Austrian territory between 1805 and 1813. Prussia dealt the French army a swift defeat in 1870, and went on to besiege the French capital causing many Parisians to die of starvation. Germany invaded France in the opening stages of both world wars. Understandably therefore, much effort since the last war has been devoted to creating political institutions, and other links, to bind the former adversaries together.

A second cause of past conflict was the so-called Eastern Question in its various forms. There was the clash between the empires of Christendom and Islam, both ideological and territorial. The assassination in Sarajevo of an Austrian archduke, and Austria's revenge for it on Serbia, provided the spark for the outbreak of the Great War. But Germany's suspicion and fear of Russia, another part of the Eastern Question, were a more fundamental cause of that war. The mutual aggression between totalitarian régimes in Germany and Russia supplied the bitterest and most costly conflict of the Second World War.

Comparatively little effort has been devoted to bringing Russia fully into the family of Western nations, or to building bridges between Christendom and Islam in Europe, and I shall return to that later. First, let us look at how efforts to resolve the conflict between France and Germany have been taken forward.

3. The Ideal of a United Europe

THE IDEAL OF CREATING A UNITED EUROPE, even a United States, grew up as part of the humanist-pacifist tradition even before the wars of the 20th century, but until the end of the second war was largely confined to academics and dreamers. Thereafter, it was taken up by statesmen like Altiero Spinelli and Jean Monnet.

The two men embodied two distinct approaches to European unity, and the distinction is important even today. Spinelli was a federalist, believing that local, regional, national and European authorities should complement each other. Monnet did not describe himself as a federalist but as a functionalist, believing that functions one by one, and therefore sovereignty, should be transferred from the national to the European level.

In the official European Community literature of the 1990s it is argued that 'Today the two approaches have been merged'.[1] Perhaps so. The Maastricht Treaty appears to owe much to a functionalist approach with its proposals that Europe should acquire its own defence and foreign policies and its own currency. But federalists will be happy with that, since the result is none the less federation, that is, the creation of a new political entity. It has the critical characteristic of a federation, in that the federation's laws are binding on the member-states.

Those who support the creation of a federation sometimes argue that federalism is generally misunderstood in Britain, and tell us that in continental Europe it is about de-centralisation, and that federal constitutions in a number of European states emphasise the devolution of powers to states or regions. But the federalism that is being unfolded at European level is not like that. It does not emphasise the devolution of powers to member-states. The process of integration now being pursued from one inter-governmental conference to the next, is highly centralising and owes much to the Monnet-functionalist approach.

British Policy on European Security

While Spinelli, Monnet and others were advancing European unity by whatever means they could, which in their day meant mostly devising institutions governing economic and trading relations in Europe, Britain held aloof from that process, but committed itself directly to European security.

There is a myth that Britain has never cared about Europe. That is an extraordinary claim. The British Empire lost nearly a million combatants in the First World War, despite beginning the war with what the Kaiser called a 'contemptibly small army'. In the Second World War, hundreds of thousands of British people died at home, or fighting in and around Europe for the freedom of Europe.

Following that war, at a time when the nature of the Soviet Empire was becoming clear, the British foreign secretary, Ernest Bevin, committed Britain to a Western Union, an alliance of

---

[1] P. Fontaine, *Europe in Ten Points*, European Communities, 1995.

European and non-European states dedicated to providing their peoples with security. In 1954, attempts to create a European Defence Community were scuppered by France at the Paris Conference. But the British foreign secretary, Anthony Eden, made an historic commitment on behalf of this country to maintain land and air forces in Europe for the following 40 years, thus providing a clear and unmistakable guarantee of Britain's willingness to fulfil its obligations if the security of our allies were ever violated. It was a remarkable undertaking for an island nation to make, especially given our traditional strategy of maintaining a small army and avoiding Continental military commitments.

Different Models for Europe

We need to understand the history in order to understand how strong is the impetus to European integration. The momentum derives from an understandable fear of war. That is what lies behind Chancellor Kohl's famous remark that European integration is 'a question of war and peace'.[2] We all subscribe wholeheartedly to the objective of achieving peace and security. More importantly, British foreign policy over five decades has been committed to that objective, and Britain's actions have followed its words.

Everyone can appreciate the terrible suffering experienced by Europe and share in the objective of never allowing it to happen again. Furthermore, Europe is right to sweep away barriers to trade, investment and mobility across the boundaries of the nation states of our Continent. But there are many different means by which those objectives can be achieved. The functionalist, that is to say, centralising model now being applied by the Commission, and by most of our partner countries, is not the only paradigm that could be used. Nor is it the case that those who oppose the present course are anti-European, still less chauvinist or xenophobic.

General de Gaulle was famously in favour of a *'Europe des patries'*, and opposed the tendency of the European Commission to acquire new powers for itself. He employed rough tactics to establish the principle that nation states should not be over-ruled by majorities on matters of vital national interest. How could it be that someone who valued Europe, who had fought for its freedom

---

[2] Helmut Kohl, speech to University of Louvain, 5 February 1996.

and knew as much as any about war, still nurtured a belief in the nation state?

The answer to that question requires us to consider a little more deeply what are the causes of conflict. It seems that those who want to create a United States of Europe believe that nationalism has been the principal cause. They think that if you can replace the nation states, and make the nations of Europe dependent on each other in a new European state, you will have dealt with the problem of nationalism and therefore abolished the main cause of war.

But it is not enough to assert that European wars have been caused by rampant nationalism. Two other things have also been necessary: despotism and a sense of grievance. Take any of the wars of the last two centuries, and it will be seen that the aggressors were despots: French revolutionaries, kaisers, emperors, Hitler and Stalin. They capitalised ruthlessly on some supposed injustice done to their nation, some piece of territory that had to be restored to the mother- or fatherland, some minority that yearned to be set free from its foreign repressor.

4. The Spread of Democracy - and of Security

THE GREAT VICTORY IN EUROPE at the end of the Second World War was the restoration of democracy in Germany and Italy, and the liberation of those countries that had been conquered by the axis powers. Subsequently Spain, Portugal and Greece rejoined the family of democratic nations. My father fought for democracy in Spain and was a refugee from tyranny for 20 years. To see democracy restored there brought my family great joy. Following the fall of the Iron Curtain, most of Eastern Europe and even Russia have become young democracies, to the joy of millions who had suffered there. Democracy is precious to everyone, but its value is most appreciated by those who know what it is to be without it.

The European Union, along with NATO and other European institutions, has played an important part in the extension of democracy through Europe. Their member-states have provided a shining example of both freedom and material success, and Western institutions have supplied the template of democratic values to be reproduced by the new democracies if they are to aspire to join them as new members. Europe is more secure from conflict within the Continent now than ever before, because there have never been so many democracies as now, and it is inconceivable that democracies would go to war with one another.

Viewed like that, democracy acquires a special value. It is not merely, as Churchill said, the worst system except for all the rest, it is *the* form of government that best assures peace. If we do not have security, we cannot hope to achieve anything decent in life, because we have seen repeatedly in Europe that without it we risk descending into absolute barbarity. Democracy provides the best guarantee of security. Without democracy, for all its alleged deficiencies, the abyss would yawn before us.

European integration is not the means to achieve the security of our Continent. It is the wrong route. Integration is being designed in a way that sharply reduces democratic control. If we shoe-horn the nations of Europe into an artificial union, we will not abolish nationalism, indeed we risk stirring it up. The danger is that we make people feel that their national interests will be overlooked, and that they cannot assert them through the ballot. That risks exactly what the architects of the new Europe say they wish to avoid: destabilising Europe, creating tensions and releasing resentments that damage the present good relations between European nations.

What Is Democracy?

Let us consider what democracy is and how it works. The origins of the word are illuminating: *demos* meaning the people or commons of an ancient Greek state and hence the populace, and *cracy* meaning rule or power. The earliest Greek democracy depended on a very small populace, those of a city, those that could be expected to gather together in one place. Their *commonality* was evident. In the modern world it is more difficult to be precise about what constitutes a *people*. It is obviously a matter of great controversy and can be subject to change. Most nation states have a common language, but not all. Many nation states have a principal nationality or ethnic group, but not all. Most nation states are geographically homogeneous, but not all. The United States of America would not score very high on any of those criteria, and yet it is undoubtedly a nation state. Its people are explicitly bound together by a clearly articulated sense of national purpose and by a set of shared values, by a vision of themselves and by a notion of

14

their place in the world. All of that provides them with the things in common that make them a people. Much the same could be said of most of the nation states of Europe, though admittedly some to a greater and others to a lesser extent.

For democracy to work, people have to have more than just a vote. They need to feel a part of the institutions to which they elect representatives. They need to feel properly represented in those bodies. They need to believe that their vote can change things.

Scottish Frustration

That can give rise to problems within nation states. It seems that a majority of Scottish people do not now feel confident on those points with regard to the parliament at Westminster. Evidently they do not feel properly represented there, sensing that Scotland has particular interests that may tend to be overlooked in London, experiencing frustration when at general elections the United Kingdom produces a different sort of government from that which Scotland alone would have selected. Whether that leads in due course to a break-up of the United Kingdom remains to be seen, and that is not within the scope of this paper. The point is that recent events in Scotland give us an indication of a mood, also to be found well beyond Scotland, about representative government. Such government must be seen to be sensitive and responsive to the way in which people perceive themselves and the sense of commonality which they feel.

The Scottish example is interesting because there is no ethnic or linguistic difference between the Scots and the English. England, Scotland and Wales are, taken together, geographically homogeneous and distinct. We three nations share many common values and sense of national identity, and yet the Scots are unhappy about certain things done in their name and decided at Westminster. People in democracies have to feel that the critical decisions that affect their daily lives are taken in a forum within which they see themselves as properly represented. The Basques, Catalonians, Bretons, Bavarians and other groups in Europe feel that too.

The important conclusion for the purposes of this lecture is that we will be storing up the causes of future resentment and unrest if policy which affects people's lives and livelihoods is made by bodies which are thought to be too distant, or made by people who are not democratically accountable at all. The sort of political decisions about which people rightly feel very strongly are those that affect the level of interest rates, taxes and unemployment.

5. The Single Currency

THAT BRINGS US TO THE SINGLE CURRENCY. Most of the remainder of this lecture is concerned with the political consequences of introducing a single currency. The economic arguments against the scheme were made brilliantly in the speech that William Hague gave to the CBI, and I concur completely. I have a few comments on the economic consequences, but I cannot improve on what he said.

The proposal to institute a single currency in Europe involves a bigger step towards centralised decision-making than any that has been taken before. It seems difficult for many people in Britain to grasp that the motivation is political, not economic. As Dr Helmut Hesse, a member of the directorate of the Bundesbank, has said, monetary union is to be seen 'as the last step in a process of integration that began only a few years after the Second World War in order to bring peace and prosperity to Europe'.[3] And Dr Hesse sees it in those clear terms even though as a banker you might expect him rather to highlight the economic significance of the change.

The responsibility for monetary policy will pass from the governments of the member-states, or from their central banks, to the European Union central bank. Member-states will be compelled also to transfer their foreign reserves from their national central banks to the European central bank. They will be required to limit their borrowing to maintain convergence. The effect of the first is to make it extremely difficult for any member-state to run a deficit, and the effect of the second is to provide for sanctions against it should it none the less succeed in doing so. It does not take much imagination to realise that a constraint on the level of borrowing in practice translates into a severe curtailment of the freedom to decide either the level of public spending or the rate of taxation.

---

[3] Helmut Hesse, speech to the Stadtsparkasse, Osnabrück, 31 October 1995,

Transfer of Monetary and Financial Policy Inevitable

The Chancellor of the Exchequer, Gordon Brown, has claimed that there is 'no question of giving up our ability to make decisions on tax and spending'. I do not know whether that owes more to naiveté or to dishonesty. I have respect for the Chairman of the Bundesbank, Hans Tietmeyer, who hides nothing when he says:

> 'a European currency will lead to member-states transferring their sovereignty over financial and wage policy, as well as in monetary affairs. It is an illusion to think that states can hold on to their autonomy over taxation policy.'[4]

The consequences have been accurately represented by Chancellor Kohl, when he said plainly: 'We want the political unification of Europe. If there is no monetary union, then there cannot be political union, and vice-versa.'[5]   Indeed, there is no currency in the world that is not controlled by a nation state, and no country of significant size that does not control its own currency.

In contrast to Chancellor Kohl, other advocates of the single currency often play down the significance of its implications. For example, they argue that there is not much difference between giving responsibility for the level of interest rates to a national central bank or passing it to a European institution. There is a huge difference. A national central bank should be responsible to the national parliament or to the government. Its role and scope are embedded within a democratic constitution. It should be set clear objectives and be held accountable for its performance. Failures can be punished by dismissal of the governor or board. The European central bank will not be responsible to any democratic body, and the single currency itself is claimed to be irreversible.

Decisions about interest rates in effect become decisions about rates of inflation and unemployment – the most sensitive of all policy matters. If people feel that in elections they are unable to give their view of economic management through their vote, or

---

[4] Quoted by Will Podmore in *The European Journal*, November 1997.

[5] Helmut Kohl, speech to the Council of Europe, 28 September 1995.

change the people who have made the policy, they will rightly feel that their democracy no longer counts for much. What will be the point of voting for political parties if they are powerless to change policy? Electors will feel resentful and cheated.

When people feel like that, they become vulnerable to extremist influences, something which we should all wish to avoid at all costs. Where democracy is working, intolerance and political extremism do not attract widespread support amongst the population. Nasty mincrities remain merely that, because the majority retains its confidence in the democratic system. The population believes that grievances can be remedied, or at least that those responsible for things that they do not like can be despatched at the polls. Once large numbers of people cease to have faith in the system, extremism can take hold, including extremist nationalism.

The Scope for Autonomy

Enthusiasts for the single currency also contend that arguments against transferring control of the currency are based on an out-of-date view of national sovereignty, since these days the scope for independent action by each country is severely constrained by economic events elsewhere. Of course we are affected by events outside our control, but considerable scope for independent action remains. The Bundesbank evidently feels that it has considerable autonomy despite the impact of global forces. In Britain's case, the point is most easily demonstrated by contrasting our experience inside the ERM (which made it impossible for us to reduce our interest rates below 10 per cent, and indeed on the last day of membership we proposed to raise them to 15 per cent) with our experience subsequently, when we were able to cut interest rates to about 5 per cent. There are degrees of freedom, and the fact that we are not totally independent of outside influences is no argument for throwing away the considerable amount of scope for action we still possess. More importantly, our *right* to make choices for ourselves should not be given up on such spurious grounds.

Following the ignominy of Britain's exit from the ERM, the British people were free to vote against the Conservatives who had taken them into it, causing the loss of many homes, businesses and jobs. If we were members of a single currency and the key decisions were taken by the European central bank, voters would no longer be able to vote out the people who made harmful economic decisions. What is more, at least in the case of the ERM it was possible, however painfully, for Britain to leave and thus to reverse policy. There is, we are told, no exit from the single currency.

6. Why Democracy Will Not Work at the European Level

SOME WHO KNOW THESE ARGUMENTS will object that democratic accountability for the European central bank's decisions could and should be established at European level through the European parliament. The point demonstrates the success that Monnet and his successors have had over the years. In the period following the war it was impossible to find many followers for the visionary notion of a United States of Europe. But the pioneers of European integration patiently made what progress they could with smaller- scale projects in the economic field, leading in due course to the idea of a single currency. The single currency, however, requires the centralisation of decision-making on issues that are so very important, that even those who oppose the whole idea may cry out for the creation of centralised democratic institutions to provide some element of people's control.

The creation of the European state has been approached in reverse order to the creation of almost any other. Normally, a new state establishes its institutions of government *first*, and goes on to create its policies and its currency. In this case, the common European policies and the currency are being created first, with the intention that that should lead to demands, in the names of logic and of democracy, for the formation of the institutions of centralised European government.

The European parliament is not presently perceived by the British people, perhaps not by any other population either, as a representative body invested with much democratic trust and authority. That is not merely because it is in its infancy. Democracy requires not only the *cracy* but also the *demos*, not only the state but also the people. You can create the apparatus of a state at European level, with a common frontier, a single immigration policy, a common foreign and defence policy, and a single currency. All the attributes of the nation state, all its *functions*, can be transferred to the European level along the Monnet-functionalist model. But what we do not have and what we cannot conjure up is a *demos* – that is, a single European people.

Diversity of European Peoples

If the Scots are now doubting that a democracy spanning from John o' Groats to Land's End is capable of making every part of the country feel properly represented, then certainly no parliament spanning from Dublin to Athens, and being charged with the critical decisions affecting our lives and livelihoods, is capable of satisfying the democratic requirements and aspirations of each of our populations.

The peoples of Europe are too different from one another, their histories, cultures and values are too diverse, for them to be brought together into one state. We can work together and co-operate for mutual benefit, but Europeans do not have a common identity, or view of their role in world affairs. They do not constitute a nation, and since they do not we should not try to create a European nation state. We should not try to do at European level things that nation states should do. Nation states should take the most sensitive policy decisions, because they require democratic control, and democracy can work only within a nation state where people share values, history and cultural tradition.

Looking Back Instead of Forward

One of the boldest efforts of propaganda by the enthusiasts for European integration, is the attempt to portray themselves as modern and forward-looking. They are the opposite. They are mainly motivated by a fear that the past may repeat itself, that is, that Franco-German rivalry or rampant German nationalism may re-awaken. They propose a centralisation of power that runs flatly in the opposite direction to the march of history. We can see around us that the old empires or unions of states have collapsed in failure. The Soviet Union and Yugoslavia both failed in their attempts, even using coercion, to sustain a centralised system of governmental control over a wide area, covering many diverse peoples and nations.

The European integrationists are out-of-date in another way too. They see a European political union as a necessary response to global competition, believing that we must react to the challenge posed by the industrial and trading giants, like the USA and Japan, by creating a giant Europe. Chancellor Kohl has claimed that 'the nation-state ... cannot solve the great problems of the twenty-first century' and that Europe has to 'assert itself'.[6] Dr Helmut Hesse has said that 'a multiplicity of small states is not suitable for the world economy today'.[7]

Global competition is indeed between industrial giants, but they are companies, not nation states. There may well be an argument for industrial mergers in Europe, for example between defence contractors in France, Germany and Britain. But that is a completely separate agenda from political integration. Paradoxically, some of the people who are spurring us on towards political union are also those who still believe in national protectionism, and therefore refuse to implement policies that would bring about European industrial rationalisation.

Big (Global) Competition, Bigger State?

Some of those who think that the right response to global competition is to create a bigger state, also believe in a bigger state in the other sense, meaning a bigger role for the state, through more interference and regulation. That frame of mind has produced the social chapter, and is a strong influence within New Labour. Such people believe that global competition will whittle away worker protection and social standards in the developed world, and that we must create a large European corral in which they can be defended against the pressures from outside.

New Labour, however, also spends a part of its time arguing against that, advocating the spread of flexible labour markets instead. In that second view they are right. Flexibility, along with rising educational standards, will enable us to compete *and* to improve our social standards. Excessive interference by governments, whether at national or European level, is clumsy and unresponsive, and has already played a large part in creating unemployment levels in Europe that are well above those of the USA.

---

[6] Helmut Kohl, speech to the University of Louvain, 5 February 1996.

[7] Helmut Hesse, speech to the Stadtsparkasse, Osnabrück, 31 October 1995.

21

We are being led towards a Europe which displays many of the characteristics of Britain 20 years ago. It is populated with over-manned and protected nationalised industries. In many places private sector managers are in thrall to trade unions. Business is tied down by government bureaucracy and interventionism. Public spending is appallingly high. There persists the belief that Europe can go its own sweet way, unaffected by the assault from international competition, provided that the fortress walls are built high enough. Twenty million unemployed Europeans give mute testimony to the failure of those policies. To present any of that as forward-looking is indeed a triumph for the spin doctors.

7. Will the Single Currency Be an Economic Success for Britain?

THERE ARE THOSE, no doubt, who would argue that even if it is true that the single currency requires the centralisation of important policy-making, and even if you cannot re-create at European level the sort of representative democracy to which we have become accustomed in our nation states, we are likely to get better decisions from a European central bank than we have had from governments in the past, and that will make people happier.

That is hard to believe. Unaccountable bureaucracy does not produce better decisions than democracy. The corruption and inefficiency in the Common Agricultural Policy sufficiently tells us that. Furthermore, there is no evidence that a single currency will lead to better policies, greater stability or greater economic success for its members. It is pure conjecture. The single currency will be traded in world markets against other currencies. Whether it is more stable than the national currencies it replaces will depend on how good are the policies of those who control it.

There has been no stability between the currencies of the USA and Japan, the world's largest and second largest economies. Currency stability is an illusion, and in Asia there is now on display many a scalp of men who declared that their currencies would hold their values.

Case for Joining Weaker

The case for Britain joining a single currency has lost whatever appeal it might have had when first presented a few years back. Five or 10 years ago it was plausible to argue that Britain was forever dogged by inflation, and doomed continually to resort to devaluation in order to maintain competitiveness. Unemployment in the UK was stubbornly high. By contrast, Germany appeared to have discovered the secret of non-inflationary growth, and was able to compete successfully in the world on the basis of quality, despite the strength of its currency. How much better, the argument went, for Britain to give up control over its own economy in order to reap the benefits of the German economic miracle.

Things look rather different now. Britain has gained control of inflation by its own efforts. Britain has lower unemployment than most of its European neighbours, and that is just one of many indicators that it is competing successfully. The current concern is not with devaluation, but with the strength of the pound.

Mr Blair has said that he wishes to decide whether to enter a single currency solely according to an assessment of whether it is in Britain's economic interest to do so. As will be clear from what I have said already, I think that misses the point of what is really involved in the decision. But anyway, the economic case appears very weak. It has been argued that the single currency is the logical completion of the single market. It is not. The greatest trading partners in the world, Canada and the USA, do not have a common currency and have no plans to establish one. At present, none of the countries with which Britain trades has the same currency as we do, and yet our trade with them goes on rising. I can see that there would be a small saving on transaction costs for companies trading with Europe if we all had the same currency, but it would be marginal. Against that, British industry has to ask itself whether it really wishes to enter the next recession with the currency locked at its present level, and with the British government powerless to vary interest rates.

'Grave Danger'

The grave danger for Europe, economically speaking, is to introduce a single currency where no single labour market exists. A single currency means that, in future, variations in economic

23

performance between one region and another cannot result, as they do today, in a downward adjustment of the currency in the less successful areas, and interest rates must reflect policy established at the centre, not local conditions. The full impact of recession will therefore fall on unemployment.

In the USA, a vast area covered by a single currency, people who lose their jobs in a depressed area can move to another state in search of a job, however inconvenient it may be. But people cannot move at will within our Continent to find new work. They face barriers related to language, qualifications, local culture and plain prejudice. Some of those can be reduced with the passage of time, but most will prove intractable. Indeed, with the so-called Posted Workers Directive, approved under the Social Chapter, European Union labour ministers seem determined to reduce labour mobility across borders.

There is another danger. Britain presently receives a notably high proportion of the inward investment attracted into Europe. Those investors clearly see value in Britain's membership of the EU and free access to its markets. But they also see it as an advantage that the British economy is more flexible and de-regulated than some others in Europe. In other words, Britain derives an advantage from not embracing all European economic policy. Investors know that wherever they invest there is an exchange rate risk. But British economic policy over the last 18 years has offered them stability and reassurance.

But if we join the Euro, economic policy in Britain will be determined principally by events in the geographical centre of the European Union. There may well be a mismatch between conditions in Britain and Germany. Interest rates could be inappropriate to British economic circumstances, as they were when we were in the ERM. That represents a bad risk for investors. It may then make more sense for them to invest where local economic conditions and interest rates are most closely related, that is, in Germany. Imagine the impact upon British public opinion if unemployment is high, and inward investors are drifting away, the government is powerless to vary interest rates, and the electorate is unable to change anything by electing a new one.

8. The Real Questions of Security

I BEGAN THIS LECTURE by recognising the importance of European security. All other objectives are secondary. The principal guarantor of peace in Europe has been NATO. It has provided a wholly credible deterrent against attack. With American troops positioned in Europe, any potential adversary was wise to believe that America really would go to war to preserve the territory of its European allies. America's awesome military capability was evident.

Incidentally, the establishment of NATO did not infringe the sovereignty of its members. Its Treaty is explicitly an agreement of sovereign states who undertake under Article 5 to regard the violation of the territory of another member-state as though it were a violation of their own and to respond with such action *as they deem necessary.* NATO has no federalist destiny. In the near half-century since it was founded, unlike the EU, it has passed no laws that bind its member-states, and no court has extended its influence. In no way has it increased its powers since 1948. The democratic accountability of governments has not been affected.

NATO is now responding to the new situation created since the end of the Cold War, recognising that the greatest contribution it can make to security is to strengthen the new democracies of Europe. Membership of either NATO or the EU or of both can help underpin those democracies. The EU should follow NATO's example. It should be trying to lower the barriers for entry by the countries of Eastern Europe, rather than creating an inner core which requires qualifications that they cannot hope to attain. Negotiating admission for new members looks like being a protracted, and maybe cantankerous, business.

The EU's Remaining Security Tasks

The EU must also address itself to the remaining security issues in our Continent. We need to do all we can to make Russia feel welcome in the family of Western democracies. Membership of either NATO or the EU is impractical, not least because Russia is a vast Asian as well as European power. But again, the EU ought to be demolishing fences rather than continuing to develop its fortress.

In the case of Turkey, the EU seems to be almost careless in its relations. The EU has made it clear to Turkey that although it applied for membership years ago, there is no early prospect of admission. Meanwhile countries that have only recently become democratic and pro-Western are politely ushered to positions higher up the queue. Few things could be more important for our security than that Turkey should remain democratic and well-disposed towards the West. Turkey is being kept at bay, partly because some European leaders apparently see the EU as a subset of Christendom; and partly because with its manifest social problems, Turkey's inclusion certainly would create substantial problems of integration. We have had to put heavy reliance on Turkey as a NATO ally during our conflicts with Iraq. It is difficult for the Turkish government to sell to its people the merits of being a good member of NATO, and it is difficult for us to persuade Turkey to be reasonable over the Cyprus problem, if it is offered so little by the EU.

Here is an instance where the EU has a clear choice between on the one hand maintaining its preoccupation with achieving 'ever closer European union', and on the other hand using its enlargement to enhance the security of its members. It appears to have made the wrong choice. It fails to think strategically.

9. Conclusion

THIS CASE SERVES TO ILLUSTRATE a broader truth. Those who are most influencing the progress of Europe have become dreadfully confused. They believe that European integration is the only guarantee of future security, and they are pursuing the objective with a single-mindedness that borders on fanaticism.

They are wrong. It is democracy that provides our greatest hope of future peace and prosperity. We should use our Atlantic and European institutions in every way we can to spread democracy and nurture it where it takes root.

The European Union is entirely made up of member-states that are democracies. But the European Union itself is not democratic. Neither the Commission, nor the Council of Ministers, nor the European central bank is democratically accountable, and neither can they be made so because Europe is not a nation. It follows that the more we transfer decision-making away from the democratic member-states to the undemocratic European Union, the less shall we enjoy democratic accountability.

Moving away from democratic control is retrograde in itself, but it is also highly dangerous, because disillusion and grievance provide a breeding ground for nationalism and extremism. In the interests of security, of tolerance and harmony between nations, in the interests of preserving the most valued gain of the post-war period which is democracy, we should turn away from the headlong rush towards European political integration, in which the single currency is a decisive step.

Postscript

Asking for Trouble:
The Single Currency Will Lead to Regional
Conflict, not Economic Efficiency*
MARTIN FELDSTEIN

THE EUROPEAN NATIONS hurtling toward economic and monetary union are heading for trouble. EMU is likely to bring higher unemployment and higher inflation. Pursuit of a common policy will cause conflicts among participating governments that will intensify as the monetary union evolves into a more wide-ranging political union responsible for foreign, military and domestic policies.

Joblessness will rise because interest and exchange rates will no longer automatically counter cyclical unemployment. Today, for example, if a recession in Latin America causes Spanish exports to decline, the peseta weakens and Spanish interest rates fall. That causes Spain's other exports to rise and domestic interest-sensitive spending to increase. The net effect is a smaller rise in unemployment. But once the peseta is replaced by the euro, Spain cannot be helped by a currency adjustment or by a fall in interest rates (since these must be uniform throughout the Monetary Union). EMU membership would also deny Spain the option of easing monetary policy to stimulate growth and employment. And, because of the misnamed stability pact, the Spanish government will not be able to cut taxes or raise spending to offset a fall in demand.

Some Europeans reject such pessimism, citing the example of the US, which avoids persistent high regional unemployment despite its single currency and single central bank.

---

* Professor Feldstein's article was first published in *Time Magazine* in the 'Viewpoint' column on 19 January 1998. Professor Feldstein is Professor of Economics at Harvard University and former Chairman of the US Council of Economic Advisers.

Unfortunately, three basic differences between the US and Europe mean that America's success with a single currency is not relevant to Europe.

First, Americans are very mobile – moving from unemployment regions to places where there are jobs. In Europe, linguistic barriers prevent similar mobility. Second, US wages are much more flexible. Wages fall in regions where demand declines, offsetting increases in production employment and, finally, when income declines, individual and business taxes paid to the federal government decline sharply, implying a strong net transfer to that region. For these reasons, unemployment rates are far less sensitive to US regional demand fluctuations than they would be in a single-currency Europe.

Europe's current double-digit unemployment rates are not cyclical but are caused by bad structural policies – misguided regulations, high minimum wages, and generous unemployment benefits. A few countries have made progress by changing these counterproductive rules. Their experience shows what can be done and provides competitive pressures to force reform elsewhere. But the increased centralisation of policy that accompanies EMU will make it harder for individual countries to experiment with reforms. The European Commission's recent pronouncement that it will force countries to respect maximum working hours is an indication of things to come.

Inflation in Europe has fallen sharply during the past decade as individual central banks emulated Germany's fiercely anti-inflationary Bundesbank. Although other countries do not share German's fervid opposition to inflation, they have been forced to follow Germany's lead to avoid devaluing their currencies. This monetary discipline will end when EMU gives every country an equal vote at the European Central Bank. Without Germany's leadership, European inflation will be higher in the next decades than it has been in recent years.

These adverse effects on unemployment and inflation far outweigh the commercial benefits that will flow from EMU. The elimination of tariffs and other barriers by the 1992 Single Market agreement was far more important for stimulating trade and investment.

Despite these shortcomings, EMU looks likely to begin on schedule because economic issues are secondary to political aspirations. For Germany and France EMU offers the possibility of dominating European policy-making. Countries like Italy and Spain will join to show that they are economically and politically worthy of membership and the smaller countries are joining to have a seat at the table where European policies are determined. The Maastricht Treaty that created the EMU calls for a European political union with broad domestic and international responsibilities. Moreover, since no significant country exists – or has ever existed – without its own currency, the shift to a single currency for the EMU members is a giant step toward such a European state.

Ever since the end of World War II a single European government has been advocated as a way of keeping the peace. But a European political union is more likely to be a source of conflict than a foundation for European harmony. There will be quarrels over monetary policy, over taxation and over the shaping of common foreign policies. There will be disputes between Germany and France about their relative power and influence. There will be conflicts that flow from the frustrations of other EU countries – including Britain if it decides to enter – when they find that they are marginalised in the decision process. A European political union with 300 million people and the ability to project miltary force around the world could be the source of broader international instability in the decades ahead.

Back From the Brink: An Appeal to Fellow Europeans Over Monetary Union

Pedro Schwartz

1. European Monetary Union is an 'unprecedented experiment', a 'huge gamble' which produces mixed reactions among Europeans.

2. There are many possible pitfalls before monetary union can come into being. One particular problem is that from 1998 to 2001, national currencies will remain legal tender. The currencies of 'misbehaving countries' may therefore be '…pounced upon by speculators and marauders…'

3. A monetary zone can function effectively only if it encompasses a single market, especially a single labour market. Establishing a monetary union when there is no hope of removing some of the barriers to a single market means '…applying perpetual fetters'.

4. The labour market of the European Union is '…far from being integrated'. The entry into monetary union of countries with rigid labour markets would warp the functioning of the union: moreover, those countries would probably demand subsidies to alleviate unemployment.

5. European Monetary Union therefore faces 'a bumpy road' before and after 2002. Before 2002 there may be 'speculative storms'; after 2002 large pockets of unemployment may persist, undermining European unity.

6. If European politicians had really wanted a stable currency they would have linked their currencies to the Deutschmark and turned their Central Banks into currency boards.

7. Monetary competition among existing European currencies plus the euro would offer a better long run prospect of monetary stability than monetary union.

8. Competitive devaluation is less of a problem than industrial lobbies claim. Over-valuation is more of a danger: '…fake converts from easy virtue love the prestige of a strong currency'.

9. In practice, careful economic analysis of European Monetary Union 'counts for nothing'. The proposed union is a 'dangerous experiment…' to build a certain kind of Europe surreptitiously' and to give a '…huge boost to centralisation'.

10. If monetary union goes ahead, Britain should go it alone and '…set an example from within the European Union of what can be achieved by a competitive, deregulated, private economy with a floating and well-managed currency'.

The Institute of Economic Affairs

2 Lord North Street, Westminster, London SW1P 3LB
Telephone: 0171 799 3745 Facsimile: 0171 799 2137
E-mail: iea@iea.org.uk Internet: http://www.iea.org.uk

ISBN 0-255 36401-6

£4.00